Cath Kidston

TEATIME

Cath Kidston®
TEATIME

50 cakes and bakes for every occasion

quadrille

Contents

Introduction

For the British it's an excuse to 'put the kettle on' and make a cup of tea, but wherever you are in the world the idea is the same. Teatime is a pause in the middle of the afternoon, time to stop what you're doing and take a break.

Perhaps a 4pm energy slump has struck and you need a reviving coffee and a little something to nibble on at your desk, maybe it's an after-school snack for the kids, or perhaps it's just an opportunity to take five minutes out of a busy day to enjoy some calm and solitude. Whatever the reason, 'teatime' has become ingrained in the fabric of our day-to-day lives.

But beyond the daily grind, teatime is also a wonderful opportunity for a get-together, whether it's a relaxed gathering with family and friends and a chance to catch up over cookies, cake and other treats, or a chance to dress the table, lay out your best crockery and celebrate a special occasion. Either way, the wonderful thing about teatime is that you can go to as much or as little trouble as you like.

The recipes in this book have been designed to cater to different teatime occasions. You'll find all the hallmarks of a classically British afternoon tea, like feather-light buttermilk scones, home-made jams and buttercream-layered cakes; pillars of bake sales and school fundraisers, such as fruity flapjacks and rich chocolate brownies; and the hearty sausage rolls, cheesy muffins and rustic tarts that are perfect for eating al fresco when tea becomes a picnic. There's also a whole chapter of celebration cakes, with lavish bakes for those occasions when you need to pull out all the stops and wow your guests.

We know that not everyone has time to spend hours in the kitchen baking, making their own pastry or creating many-tiered party cakes (we certainly don't!), so we've kept things pretty simple. All easy to prepare, these recipes are aimed at the novice baker, with plenty of tips and expert advice throughout. Let our pretty, modern vintage range of bakeware, china and fabrics inspire your presentation, decoration and table setting, serve your bakes piled high and gather your guests round for a proper afternoon spread. Oh, and don't forget to pop the kettle on!

Afternoon
tea

Afternoon tea

Today's busy lives mean that the British tradition of sitting down to afternoon tea every day is no longer a realistic (or particularly healthy!) proposition. The afternoon 'snack' of sandwiches and dainty cakes was originally created to help the peckish Duchess of Bedfordshire bridge the gap between lunch and dinner. Yet the idea behind it – that pause in the day – is still a wonderful excuse for a gathering; a chance to bring friends and family together over scones and jam, generous cakes and steaming pots of tea.

The traditional teatime fare you'll find in this chapter is designed to be simple to prepare and doesn't require you to be an experienced baker to serve up a sumptuous spread. From classic buttermilk scones and a Victoria sandwich, to a Dorset apple cake and a Welsh bara brith fruitcake, these are delicious, comforting bakes, best served piled high with bottomless pots of tea.

Victoria sandwich with vanilla cream and macerated strawberries

SERVES 12

200g (¾ cup, plus 2 tbsp) unsalted butter, softened, plus extra for greasing

200g (1 cup) caster (superfine) sugar

pinch of salt

4 medium eggs, beaten

200g (1½ cups) self-raising flour

1 tsp baking powder

1–2 tbsp milk

1 tsp vanilla extract

For the macerated strawberries

400g (4 cups) strawberries, hulled and cut in half

40g (3¼ tbsp) caster (superfine) sugar

For the vanilla cream

300ml (1¼ cups) double (heavy) cream

1 tsp vanilla extract

icing (powdered) sugar, to serve

Preheat the oven to 180°C/350°F/gas 4. Grease and line two 20cm (8in) sandwich tins with baking parchment.

In a large bowl, beat the butter until soft. Add the sugar and salt and beat until the mixture is very pale and fluffy. Gradually add the egg, a little at a time, beating well after each addition. Sift over the flour and baking powder in two additions and fold into the mixture using a large metal spoon until just combined. Very gently fold in the vanilla and 1 tablespoon of the milk, adding more of the milk, if necessary, to loosen.

Divide the mixture between the tins, smooth the surface with a spatula, then bake for 20–25 minutes, until golden and the cake springs back when lightly pressed. Allow the cakes to cool in their tins for 10 minutes, then turn out on to a cooling rack and leave to cool completely.

Meanwhile, tip the strawberries into a bowl and sprinkle over the sugar. Leave for 20 minutes or so, until the strawberries are juicy and slightly softened.

Once the cakes are completely cool, whip the cream with the vanilla in a large bowl until it forms soft peaks. Dollop the cream on to one of the cakes and use a palette knife to spread it out almost to the edges. Spoon over two thirds of the strawberries in an even layer and top with the other sponge. Dust with icing sugar, then spoon the remaining strawberries on top.

This cake is best eaten fresh but will keep in the fridge for up to 2 days. If refrigerating, allow the cake to come to room temperature before serving.

Lemon and poppy seed drizzle cake

SERVES 8

125ml (½ cup) warm milk

2 tbsp poppy seeds

grated zest of 3 lemons, plus the juice of 1

200g (¾ cup, plus 2 tbsp) unsalted butter, softened, plus extra for greasing

200g (1 cup) caster (superfine) sugar

3 medium eggs, lightly beaten

200g (1½ cups) self-raising flour

For the icing

150g (1 cup) icing (powdered) sugar

grated zest and juice of 1 lemon

Preheat the oven to 180°C/350°F/gas 4. Grease and line a 900g (2lb) loaf tin with baking parchment. In a small bowl, mix the warm milk with the poppy seeds and set aside.

In a large bowl, beat the butter and caster sugar together until very pale and fluffy. Gradually add the egg, a little at a time, beating well after each addition.

Sift over the flour and carefully fold into the egg, butter and sugar mixture until just incorporated. Fold through the milk, poppy seeds, lemon zest and juice. Pour the mixture into the tin and bake for 40–45 minutes, until the cake is golden and a skewer inserted into the centre comes out clean.

Leave the cake to cool for a few minutes in the tin before turning out on to a wire rack to cool completely.

To make the icing, sift the sugar into a bowl and pour in the lemon juice and zest. Gradually mix the sugar into the juice until you have a fairly runny, smooth, pourable mixture – you may need to add a little more lemon juice or a little water if necessary to get the right consistency. Drizzle over the cake to serve. The cake can be kept in an airtight container for up to 3 days.

Cherry Bakewell cake

SERVES 12

175g (¾ cup) unsalted butter, plus extra for greasing

175g (¾ cup, plus 2 tbsp) caster (superfine) sugar

3 medium eggs, lightly beaten

200g (2 cups) ground almonds

100g (¾ cup) self-raising flour

1 tsp baking powder

1 tsp vanilla extract

4–6 tbsp milk

250g (1⅓ cup) cherries, stoned (if cherries are out of season, use the equivalent weight of raspberries)

25g (⅓ cup) flaked almonds

icing (powdered) sugar, to dust

Preheat the oven to 180°/350°F/gas 4. Grease and line a deep 20cm (8in) cake tin with baking parchment and set aside.

In a large bowl, beat the butter, until soft, then add the sugar. Beat together until very pale, light and fluffy. Gradually add the egg, beating well after each addition. Sprinkle over the ground almonds, breaking up any lumps as you go, and carefully fold through the mixture to combine.

Sift over the flour and baking powder, spoon over the vanilla and fold again until the mixture is just combined. If the mixture is looking a little dry, add enough of the milk to loosen. Briefly stir through the cherries and pour the mixture into the tin. Smooth the top with a spatula and sprinkle over the flaked almonds. Bake for 30–35 minutes, until the top is golden and a skewer inserted into the centre comes out clean.

Allow the cake to cool in the tin for 10 minutes before transferring to a wire rack to cool completely. Serve dusted with icing sugar. This cake will keep in an airtight container for up to 2 days.

Almond and elderflower cake with gooseberry cream

SERVES 12

250g (1 cup, plus 2 tbsp) unsalted butter, softened, plus extra for greasing
200g (1 cup) caster (superfine) sugar
4 medium eggs, separated
100g (¾ cup) self-raising flour
120g (1¼ cups) ground almonds
1 tsp baking powder
4 tbsp elderflower cordial
finely grated zest of 1 lemon

For the filling
250g (2 cups) gooseberries, topped and tailed (if gooseberries aren't in season, use 8 tbsp of gooseberry conserve and omit the sugar)
50g (¼ cup) caster (superfine) sugar
400ml (1¾ cups) double (heavy) cream
4 tbsp elderflower cordial

Preheat the oven to 180°C/350°F/gas 4. Lightly grease and line two 20cm (8in) sandwich tins with baking parchment.

Place the butter and sugar in a large mixing bowl and beat until very pale and fluffy. Gradually add the egg yolks, beating well after each addition. Sift over the flour, ground almonds and baking powder and gently fold through the mixture until just incorporated. Pour in the cordial, sprinkle over the lemon zest and fold through, being careful not to over-mix.

Whisk the egg whites in a clean bowl until they form soft peaks. Spoon a third of the egg white on top of the cake batter and very gently fold through to loosen the mixture. Carefully fold in the remaining egg white, a third at a time, until just combined. Divide the mixture between the two tins and level each out with a spatula. Bake for 25–30 minutes, until the cakes are golden and a skewer inserted into the centre comes out clean. Leave the cakes to cool in their tins for 10 minutes before turning out on to a wire rack to cool completely.

To make the filling, if you are using fresh gooseberries, tip them into a small saucepan with the caster sugar and a tablespoon of water. Place over

a low heat and stir until the gooseberries begin to pop. Once the sugar has dissolved and the gooseberries have broken down, set aside to cool.

Pour the cream and cordial into a mixing bowl and beat until the cream just holds its shape. Place one of the cakes on a serving plate and spoon on half of the gooseberry cream. Spread the cream almost to the edge of the cake then gently drizzle two thirds of the gooseberries or the gooseberry conserve over it. Top with the second cake and spread the remainder of the cream over it, then drizzle over the remaining gooseberry mixture. This cake can be kept for up to 3 days in the fridge – allow it to come to room temperature before serving.

Variation

Play around with the type of berry according to what's in season. Raspberries would work well but as they are naturally sweeter than gooseberries you should add the sugar slowly and taste as you go (if the berries are sweet enough you may not need any at all).

150g (1⅓ cups) pecan halves, plus 12 extra to decorate

200g (¾ cup, plus 2 tbsp) unsalted butter, melted

200g (1 cup) soft light brown sugar

4 medium eggs, lightly beaten

250g (1¾ cup, plus 2 tbsp) self-raising flour

pinch of salt

1½ tsp bicarbonate of soda (baking soda)

1 tsp ground cinnamon

½ tsp ground mixed spice

finely grated zest of 1 orange

100g (¾ cup) sultanas (golden raisins)

250g (2 cups) carrots, scrubbed and grated

For the icing

120g (½ cup) unsalted butter, softened

300g (1⅓ cups) cream cheese, at room temperature

½ tsp vanilla extract

1 tsp ground cinnamon

100g (¾ cup, minus ½ tbsp) icing (powdered) sugar

Preheat the oven to 180°/350°F/gas 4. Grease and line two 20cm (8in) cake tins with baking parchment and set aside.

Scatter the pecans over a baking tray and place in the oven. Roast the nuts for 5 minutes or so, until golden, then tip the nuts on to a plate and allow to cool before roughly chopping. Set aside.

Pour the melted butter into a large mixing bowl. Add the sugar and eggs and beat until the mixture is pale and has almost doubled in volume.

Sift the flour, salt, bicarbonate of soda and spices over the cake mix and gently fold in the dry ingredients until just combined. Carefully fold through the orange zest, sultanas, carrots and pecans, until evenly combined.

Divide the mixture between the two tins and smooth each surface with a spatula. Bake in the oven for 30–35 minutes, until the cakes are golden and a skewer inserted into the middle comes out clean. Leave to cool in the tins

for 10 minutes before turning out on to a wire rack. Allow the cakes to cool completely before icing.

To make the icing, tip the butter into a bowl and beat well until light and fluffy. Add the cream cheese, vanilla and cinnamon and beat until combined. Sift over the icing sugar and beat briefly until just incorporated – you don't want to go beyond this point as over-beating will cause it to go runny.

Scoop half of the icing on to one of cakes and smooth out with a palette knife until the icing almost reaches the edges of the cake. Top with the other cake and spread the remaining icing over the top. Decorate with the extra pecans. The cake will keep in an airtight container for up to 3 days.

Variation

For a lighter cake you could replace the carrots with the same weight of courgettes (zucchini) – you will simply need to squeeze the grated courgettes in a tea towel to remove their excess water.

Dorset apple cake with a sugar crunch topping

SERVES 12

400g (4 cups) Bramley or Granny Smith apples, peeled, cored and chopped into 1cm (½in) dice

215g (1 cup, plus 1 tbsp) golden caster (superfine) sugar

finely grated zest and juice of 1 lemon

200g (¾ cup, plus 2 tbsp) unsalted butter, at room temperature

3 large eggs, lightly beaten

175g (1⅓ cups) self-raising flour

1½ tsp baking powder

50g (½ cup) ground almonds

100g (¾ cup) sultanas (golden raisins)

2 tbsp demerara (turbinado) sugar

crème fraîche, cream or custard, to serve (optional)

Preheat the oven to 180°C/350°F/gas 4. Grease and line a 23cm (9in) deep springform cake tin with baking parchment.

Tip the chopped apple into a bowl, sprinkle over 15g (4 tsp) of the caster sugar, then add the lemon zest and juice. Give it a good stir and set aside.

Place the butter in a large mixing bowl and beat to soften. Add the remaining sugar and beat until the mixture is very pale and fluffy. Add the eggs, a little at a time, beating well after each addition. Sift over the flour, baking powder and ground almonds and fold in until just combined.

Drain the apple and add it to the cake mix, along with the sultanas. Fold through and spoon into the prepared tin. Smooth the top with a spatula and sprinkle over the demerara sugar.

Transfer to the oven and bake for 50 minutes to 1 hour, until the cake is golden, well risen and a skewer inserted into the centre comes out clean. Check the cake after 40 minutes; if it is looking too golden, cover loosely with foil and return to the oven. Leave to cool in the tin for 10 minutes before carefully removing. The cake is delicious served warm with crème fraîche, cream or custard. It can be kept in an airtight container for up to 3 days.

Buttermilk scones with sour cherries

SERVES 12

350g (2⅔ cups) self-raising flour, plus extra to dust
pinch of salt
1 tsp baking powder
90g (1⅓ cups, plus 2 tsp) unsalted butter, cubed

25g (2 tbsp) caster (superfine) sugar
60g (⅓ cup) dried sour cherries, roughly chopped (optional)
175ml (¾ cup) buttermilk
1 egg, beaten with 1 tbsp milk, to glaze

Preheat the oven to 220°C/435°F/gas 7. Sift the flour into a large bowl with salt and baking powder. Tip in the butter and lightly rub in with your fingertips until the mixture looks like fine breadcrumbs. Stir in the sugar and the dried cherries, if using.

Heat the buttermilk until just warm. Using a wooden spoon, make a well in the centre of the dry mix, pour in the buttermilk and use a table knife to mix quickly and lightly until the dough just comes together.

Sprinkle a little flour on to your work surface and tip the dough out. Gently turn it over a couple of times to smooth it out, then carefully pat the dough into a circle about 3–4cm (1–1½in) deep. Take a 5cm (2in) cutter and dip it into some flour. Plunge the cutter into the dough without twisting it and cut out as many scones as you can. Gently re-shape any remaining dough from the offcuts and continue to stamp scones out.

Transfer the scones to a baking tray and brush the tops with the egg glaze. Bake for 10–12 minutes, until the scones are well risen, golden, and the sides feel set.

Serve the scones warm from the oven with jam and clotted cream. They will keep in an airtight container for up to 2 days.

(pictured overleaf)

Raspberry and rose water jam

MAKES AROUND THREE 370G (13 OZ) JARS

1kg (2lb 3oz) raspberries (fresh or frozen)
juice of ½ lemon

1kg (2lb 3oz) granulated sugar
2 tbsp rose water (optional)

Start by sterilising your jars. Preheat the oven to 170°C/320°F/gas 3½. Once hot, place three clean 370g (13 oz) jars on their sides in the oven for 10 minutes – put the lids in the oven too. Turn off the oven, leaving the jars inside until your jam is ready. Place 2–3 saucers in the freezer to chill.

Tip half of the raspberries into a preserving or very large saucepan and add the lemon juice. Cook the raspberries over a medium heat for 3–4 minutes, until they're just beginning to break down. Add the remaining raspberries and the sugar and stir over a very low heat for 5–10 minutes, until the sugar has dissolved. Once the sugar has completely dissolved, increase the heat and bring to a vigorous boil for 5 minutes, stirring occasionally.

Remove the pan from the heat and drop a little jam on to a saucer from the freezer. Push your finger into it – it should wrinkle and look like jam. If it doesn't, return the pan to the heat and boil the mixture for another 2 minutes, then test again.

When the setting point has been reached, stir through the rose water, if using, and carefully pour the jam into the warm jars and seal with the lids. If stored in a cool, dark place, the jam can be kept unopened for up to a year. Once open, store in the fridge.

(pictured overleaf)

Walnut soda bread

SERVES 12

250g (1¾ cups, plus 2 tbsp) plain (all-purpose) flour
250g (2 cups) wholemeal (whole wheat) flour
25g (2 tbsp) unsalted butter, cubed
100g (¾ cup) porridge oats (oatmeal)

1 tsp bicarbonate of soda (baking soda)
1 tsp salt
500ml (2 cups) buttermilk or natural yogurt
100g (1 cup) walnut halves

Preheat the oven to 200°C /400°F/gas 6.

Sift both types of flour into a large bowl and using your fingertips, rub the butter into the flour until evenly combined and there are no lumps of butter. Stir through the oats, bicarbonate of soda and salt.

Using a wooden spoon, make a well in the centre of the dry mixture, pour in the buttermilk or yogurt and quickly and lightly bring the mixture together to make a rough, sticky dough. Stir through the walnuts.

Using your hands, form the mixture into a ball and transfer to a lightly-floured baking sheet. Press the top of the bread down to flatten slightly and, using the handle of the wooden spoon that has been dipped in flour, create a cross shape by pressing the handle into the dough.

Transfer to the oven and bake for 40–45 minutes, until the bread is golden and sounds hollow when tapped underneath. Keep an eye on the bread after 30 minutes – if it looks at all dark, turn the loaf over and loosely cover with foil before returning to the oven. Allow to cool on a wire rack, covered with a tea towel (this helps keep the crust quite soft). Serve either simply buttered, or as open sandwiches with one of the serving suggestions.

(pictured overleaf)

Clotted cream shortbread

MAKES 34 ROUNDS

225g (1 cup) unsalted butter, at room temperature

75g (⅓ cup) clotted cream (or the same quantity of butter, if unavailable)

130g (⅔ cup) caster (superfine) sugar, plus extra to finish

275g (2 cups) plain (all-purpose) flour, plus extra to dust

175g (1⅓ cups) rice flour

Tip the butter, cream and sugar into the bowl of a food processor and blitz until smooth. Add the flours and pulse until the mixture just comes together. Form the dough into a disc, wrap in cling film (plastic wrap) and chill in the fridge for up to 30 minutes.

Lightly flour a work surface. Gently roll out the mixture until it is about 1cm (½in) thick. Using a 5cm (2in) cutter, cut the dough into rounds. Gently bring any remaining scraps of dough together and stamp out more rounds until all the dough has been used up.

Lay the rounds on a baking sheet lined with baking parchment and chill for another 15–30 minutes, until firm. Meanwhile, preheat the oven to 160°C/325°F/gas 3.

Bake the biscuits for 25–30 minutes, until golden and sandy in texture, then transfer to a wire rack to cool. Sprinkle with more sugar to serve.

Blackberry and apple crumble cake

SERVES 12

2 Bramley apples (or 3 Granny Smiths)

250g (2 cups) blackberries

juice of ½ lemon

250g (1¼ cups) caster (superfine) sugar

½ tsp ground cinnamon

250g (1 cup, plus 2 tbsp) unsalted butter, softened, plus extra to grease

4 medium eggs, lightly beaten

300g (2¼ cups) self-raising flour

1 tsp vanilla extract

icing sugar, to dust

crème fraîche, to serve (optional)

For the crumble topping

140g (1 cup, plus 1 tbsp) plain (all-purpose) flour

80g (⅓ cup, plus 2 tbsp) cold butter, cut into small cubes

50g (¼ cup) caster (superfine) sugar

½ tsp ground cinnamon

Preheat the oven to 160°C/325°F/gas 3. Grease and line a 23cm (9in) springform tin with baking parchment.

Begin by making the topping. Tip the flour into a mixing bowl. Add the butter and gently rub it into the flour using your fingertips, until the mixture resembles large breadcrumbs and there are no lumps of butter. Stir through the sugar and cinnamon and set aside.

Peel, core and halve the apples, then cut them into 1cm (½in) cubes. Transfer the apple to a bowl and toss through the blackberries, lemon juice, 2 tablespoons of the caster sugar and the cinnamon. Set aside.

In a separate bowl, beat the butter and remaining sugar until very pale and fluffy. Gradually add the egg, a little at a time, beating well after each addition. Sift over the flour and carefully fold it into the mixture until just incorporated.

Add the vanilla, along with the fruit mixture, and gently fold everything together until just combined. Scrape the mixture into the prepared tin

and smooth the top with a spatula. Sprinkle over the crumble topping and roughly level it out. Bake the cake in the oven for 1¼–1½ hours, until golden and a skewer inserted into the centre comes out clean. Keep an eye on the cake after it has been in the oven for 1 hour – if the top is looking at all dark, cover it with a loose layer of foil before returning to the oven.

Leave the cake to cool in the tin for 10 minutes before carefully removing and transferring to a wire rack to cool completely. Dust with icing sugar to serve. This cake is delicious served with crème fraîche. The cake can be kept in an airtight container for up to 2 days.

Vanilla plum upside-down cake

SERVES 12

250g (1 cup, plus 2 tbsp) unsalted butter, plus extra for greasing
250g (1¼ cups) caster (superfine) sugar
4 medium eggs, lightly beaten
250g (1¾ cups, plus 2 tbsp) self-raising flour
1 tsp baking powder
75g (¾ cup) ground almonds
1 tsp vanilla bean paste
100g (½ cup) natural yogurt

For the topping
30g (2 tbsp) unsalted butter
30g (2 tbsp) soft light brown sugar
½ tsp vanilla bean paste
600g (1lb 5oz) ripe plums, halved, stoned and cut into 1cm- (½in-) thick slices

Preheat the oven to 180°C/350°F/gas 4. Grease and line a 23cm (9in) springform tin with baking parchment.

Begin by making the topping. Place the butter and sugar in a small saucepan over a low heat. Stir continuously until the sugar has dissolved and you have a thick caramel mixture. Stir in the vanilla paste and pour the mixture on to the bottom of the lined tin in as even a layer as possible. Lay the plum slices over the caramel in concentric circles, overlapping them. Set aside.

Beat the butter in a large mixing bowl until soft, then add the sugar and beat until the mixture is pale and fluffy. Add the egg, a little at a time, beating well after each addition. Sift over the flour, baking powder and ground almonds and fold through gently. Add the vanilla and yogurt and fold through until just incorporated. Spoon the mixture over the plums and smooth the surface.

Bake for 45–55 minutes, until the cake is golden, risen and a skewer inserted into the centre comes out clean. Allow to cool in the tin for 10 minutes, then run a knife around the edges of the tin to loosen any sticky bits of caramel. Invert the cake on to a serving plate to reveal the plums. Delicious served warm, the cake will also keep in an airtight container for up to 2 days.

Lady Grey Welsh bara brith

SERVES 12

350g (2½ cups) mixed raisins, currants and sultanas (golden raisins)
200g (1 cup) soft light brown sugar
finely grated zest of 1 orange
250ml (1 cup) hot, strong Lady Grey tea
300g (2¼ cups) self-raising flour

50g (½ cup) ground almonds
1½ tsp mixed spice
½ tsp ground cinnamon
2 medium eggs, lightly beaten
60g (¼ cup) unsalted butter, melted, plus extra for greasing

Tip the dried fruits, sugar and orange zest into a mixing bowl and pour over the hot tea. Give everything a good stir, cover and leave to soak overnight.

The following day, preheat the oven to 160°C/325°F/gas 3. Grease and line a 900g (2lb) loaf tin with baking parchment and set aside.

Sift the flour, almonds and spices over the fruits and stir gently to combine. Add the eggs and butter and beat gently until everything is just combined.

Spoon the mixture into the tin, smooth the surface with a spatula and bake for 1-1¼ hours, until golden and cooked through. Check the cake after 40 minutes – if it is looking too golden at this stage, cover loosely with foil and return to the oven.

Allow the cake to cool in the tin for 10 minutes before turning out on to a wire rack. This cake is delicious served warm with butter and will keep in an airtight container for 4-5 days.

Bitter marmalade and clementine cake

SERVES 12

200g (¾ cup, plus 2 tbsp) unsalted butter, plus extra for greasing
200g (1 cup) caster (superfine) sugar
4 medium eggs, lightly beaten
175g (1⅓ cups) self-raising flour
50g (½ cup) ground almonds
1 tsp baking powder

2 clementines
7 tbsp Seville orange marmalade
crème fraîche, to serve (optional)

For the topping
4 tbsp demerara (turbinado) sugar
3 clementines, finely sliced

Preheat the oven to 180°C/350°F/gas 4. Grease and line a 23cm (9in) springform tin with baking parchment. Sprinkle the demerara sugar evenly over the base of the tin and arrange the clementine slices over it in concentric circles, overlapping slightly. Set aside.

Beat the butter and sugar together until very pale, light and fluffy. Gradually add the egg, beating well after each addition. Sift over the flour, ground almonds and baking powder and gently fold into the mixture until just combined. Add the juice of 1 of the clementines, the finely grated zest of both and 2 tablespoons of the marmalade. Briefly stir into the mixture before spooning into the tin. Smooth the surface and bake for 40–45 minutes, until the cake is golden and a skewer inserted into the centre comes out clean. Have a look at the cake after 30 minutes – if it is looking too golden, loosely cover with foil and return to the oven. Allow the cake to cool in the tin for about 10 minutes, before turning out on to a wire rack or serving plate.

To make a glaze for the cake, gently heat the juice of the remaining clementine in a small pan. Add the remaining marmalade and allow to melt. When the marmalade has completely dissolved, bring it to the boil and simmer for 1 minute, until slightly thickened, before pouring the glaze over the cake. This cake is best served warm with crème fraîche but it will keep in an airtight container for up to 2 days.

Picnic teas

Picnic teas

The promise of an 'al fresco' tea is the ideal reason to get outdoors, go for a ramble in the countryside or a walk in the park, seek out a suitable spot to lay down a rug and spread out your wares.

Picnics call for simple, portable fare, so we've packed this chapter with things you can hold in your hands, transport easily and don't need to slice or dish out on to plates. There are sausage rolls and rustic vegetable tarts, macaroni cheese muffins and a crunchy almond brittle that will survive even the most energetic of walks. And if the sun does shine (fingers crossed!) and you're in need of a thirst-quencher, there are recipes for a refreshing rose lemonade and a home-made elderflower and lemon cordial.

Caramelised onion, thyme and feta tarts

MAKES 6

40g (3 tbsp) unsalted butter
4 medium red onions, finely sliced
1 tbsp thyme leaves, finely chopped
2 tbsp soft light brown sugar
2 tbsp balsamic vinegar

plain (all-purpose) flour, to dust
1 x 320g (11oz) sheet ready-rolled all-butter puff pastry
100g (¾ cup) feta cheese, crumbled

Preheat the oven to 200°C/400°F/gas 6.

Heat the butter in a large frying pan over a low–medium heat. Once foaming, add the onions and thyme and cook, stirring often, for 20 minutes, until the onions are completely soft and translucent. If the mixture is catching during cooking at all, add a few tablespoons of water and continue to cook. Add the sugar and vinegar and cook, stirring, for another 2–3 minutes, until slightly caramelised. Remove from the heat and set aside to cool.

Lightly dust a work surface with flour and lay the puff pastry sheet over it. Cut the pastry into 6 equal squares. Using the tip of a knife, score a line 1cm (½in) in from the edge of each square. Pile the onion mixture on to the squares within the line and sprinkle over the feta. Transfer to the oven and bake for 10-12 minutes, until the pastry is golden and crisp and the feta has coloured.

The tarts are best served warm or at room temperature. They can be kept in the fridge for up to 2 days but leave them to come back up to room temperature before serving, or re-heat in an oven set at 180°C/350° F/gas 4 for 5–6 minutes.

(pictured overleaf)

To vary your tart topping or make a selection of different tarts for your picnic, try:

- Finely sliced pears with crumbled Roquefort and chopped walnuts

- Sliced cherry tomatoes, torn mozzarella, a sprinkling of balsamic vinegar and basil

- Mascarpone, figs and Parma ham

2 tsp olive oil

4 spring onions, finely sliced

1 tbsp caramelised red onion chutney

100g (3½ cups) rocket (arugula) leaves

250g (2 cups) cooked beetroot, sliced

6 medium eggs, lightly beaten

a small handful of dill, finely chopped

120g (¾ cup) feta cheese, crumbled

salt and freshly ground black pepper

Preheat the oven to 180°C/350°F/gas 4. Line a 30 x 20cm (12 x 8in) baking tin with baking parchment.

Heat the olive oil in a small frying pan and add the spring onion. Cook for 3–4 minutes, until softened, then add the chutney and rocket. Stir for 30 seconds and as soon as the rocket is beginning to wilt, immediately remove the pan from the heat and spread the mixture evenly over the base of the tin. Layer over the beetroot slices.

Season the beaten eggs with salt and pepper, stir through the dill, then pour the mixture over the beetroot. Scatter over the feta and carefully transfer the tin to the oven. Bake for 20–25 minutes, until the frittata is golden and set. Allow the frittata to cool before cutting it into 8 slices. You could also keep it in the fridge until ready to serve.

Stilton cheese straws

MAKES 30–34

190g (1½ cups, minus 1 tbsp) plain (all-purpose) flour, plus extra to dust
a pinch of salt
110g (½ cup) cold unsalted butter, cut into small dice

150g (1⅔ cups) Stilton cheese, crumbled
¼ tsp English mustard or a pinch of English mustard powder
1 medium egg yolk, from the fridge

Sift the flour and salt into a mixing bowl. Using your fingertips, rub the butter into the flour, until the mixture resembles breadcrumbs. Alternatively, whizz in a food processor.

Stir in the cheese, mustard and the egg yolk. Add 1–2 tablespoons of cold water and mix to a firm dough. Wrap in cling film (plastic wrap) and chill in the fridge for 30 minutes.

Preheat the oven to 190°C/ 375°F/gas 5 and line a baking tray with baking parchment.

Lightly dust a work surface with flour and roll out the dough to a square about 5mm (¼in) thick. Cut the square in half, then cut each half into 1cm (½in) strips. Carefully transfer the strips on to the prepared baking tray and bake for 10–15 minutes, until crisp and golden. Leave to cool slightly on the baking tray before transferring to a wire rack to cool completely. The straws can be kept in an airtight container for 2–3 days.

450g (1lb) good-quality sausage meat
2 tbsp sage leaves, finely chopped
1 tbsp wholegrain mustard
plain (all-purpose) flour, for dusting

1 x 320g (11oz) sheet ready-rolled all-butter puff pastry
1 medium egg, beaten
cracked black pepper, for sprinkling (optional)

Preheat the oven to 200°C/400°F/gas 6. Line two baking sheets with baking parchment.

Tip the sausage meat into a large mixing bowl and add the sage and mustard. Give everything a vigorous stir with a wooden spoon until the mustard and sage are well dispersed throughout the meat.

Lightly dust a work surface with flour and lay the pastry sheet on top. Cut the sheet in half lengthways. Spread half the sausage meat along the length of one of the pastry pieces, shaping it into a sausage and leaving a 1–2cm (½–1in) gap at the edge. Brush the edge of the pastry with a little of the beaten egg and roll it around the sausage meat – pressing down the edges to secure (leave the short ends open). Trim the edges to neaten and repeat with the other half of the pastry and sausage meat.

Cut each cylinder into 6 equal pieces and brush the tops with some beaten egg. Sprinkle over a little black pepper, if using, and transfer the sausage rolls to the baking sheets – leaving at least a 2cm (1in) gap between them.

Bake in the oven for 15–20 minutes, until the pastry is crisp and golden. To check that the meat is cooked through, insert a skewer into the centre of one of the rolls for 10 seconds – if it comes out piping hot, the rolls are cooked. Leave to cool a little if transporting, or serve warm or at room temperature. The sausage rolls will keep in the fridge for up to 2 days – allow them to come back to room temperature before serving.

Asparagus and ham rolls

MAKES 6

plain (all-purpose) flour, to dust
1 x 320g (11oz) sheet ready-rolled all-butter puff pastry
120g (½ cup) garlic and herb soft cheese

100g (1 cup) fine asparagus spears
3 slices Parma ham, cut in half lengthways
1 egg, beaten
10g (1 tbsp) Parmesan cheese, finely grated

Preheat the oven to 200°C/400°F/gas 6. Line two baking sheets with baking parchment.

Lightly dust a work surface with flour and lay the puff pastry sheet out over it. Cut the pastry into 6 equal squares.

Spread a sixth of the soft cheese diagonally along the centre of each square. Take a sixth of the asparagus spears and wrap them in one of the pieces of ham. Lay the ham-wrapped asparagus over the soft cheese. Pull the two opposite corners of pastry over the filling and brush the pastry with the beaten egg to seal. Repeat with the other squares then sprinkle the rolls with the Parmesan.

Transfer the rolls to the prepared baking sheets and bake for 15–20 minutes, until the pastry is crisp and golden. The rolls can be served warm or at room temperature. Alternatively, they can be kept in the fridge for up to 2 days.

Cheese and Marmite® muffins

MAKES 12

200g (1½ cups) self-raising flour
125g (1⅓ cups) extra mature Cheddar cheese
4 spring onions (green onions), finely sliced
1 tbsp Marmite® yeast extract, plus 1 tsp

75g (⅓ cup) unsalted butter, melted
200ml (¾ cup) milk
1 large egg, lightly beaten

Preheat the oven to 190°C/375°F/gas 5. Line a 12-hole muffin tray with cases.

Combine the flour with 100g (1 cup) of the cheese and the spring onions. Set aside. In another bowl, mix the tablespoon of yeast extract into the melted butter until it dissolves. Add the milk and egg and whisk everything together to combine.

Make a well in the centre of the flour mixture and pour in the wet ingredients. Gently fold together until just combined.

Use an ice-cream scoop or large spoon to fill the muffin cases about two thirds full with the mixture. Mix the remaining cheese with the teaspoon of yeast extract and sprinkle a little over each muffin. Bake for 25–30 minutes, until the muffins are risen and golden and a skewer inserted into the centre comes out clean. The muffins can be kept in an airtight container for up to 3 days.

Macaroni cheese muffins

MAKES 12

250g (2 cups) macaroni
70g (½ cup) diced pancetta
20g (1½ tbsp) unsalted butter, plus extra for greasing
40g (¼ cup, heaped) plain (all-purpose) flour

450ml (2 cups) milk
50g (½ cup) cream cheese
½ tsp English mustard
275g (3 cups) Cheddar cheese, grated
25g (½ cup) breadcrumbs

Preheat the oven to 190°C/375°F/gas 5. Lightly grease a 12-hole muffin tin with butter.

Tip the macaroni into a large saucepan of lightly salted boiling water and simmer for 5 minutes. Drain and set aside.

Meanwhile, add the pancetta to a frying pan (adding it to a cold pan will help to render more fat) and place over a medium heat. Fry, stirring occasionally, for about 5 minutes, until the pancetta is crisp and golden brown. Add the butter to the pan and once it is foaming, add the flour. Stir for 1–2 minutes to cook the flour, before removing from the heat. Gradually pour in the milk, stirring all the time, until you have a fairly thin sauce.

Return the pan to the heat and cook gently, still stirring, until the sauce is thick and bubbling. Remove from the heat and stir through the cream cheese, mustard and 250g (2¾ cups) of the Cheddar, until the cheese has melted. Add the macaroni and give everything a good stir to combine.

Fill each hole in the muffin tin nearly to the top, then sprinkle over the remaining Cheddar, along with the breadcrumbs. Bake for 12–15 minutes, until golden and bubbling. Leave the muffins to cool in their tins for 20 minutes, before carefully removing. Once at room temperature, these muffins will be easily transportable and can be kept in the fridge for up to 2 days.

Apple and pecan turnovers

MAKES 6

30g (2 tbsp) unsalted butter
50g (½ cup) pecans, roughly chopped
350g (3½ cups) Bramley or Granny Smith apples, peeled, cored and chopped into 1cm dice
70g (⅓ cup) soft light brown sugar

plain (all-purpose) flour, to dust
1 x 320g (11oz) sheet ready-rolled all-butter puff pastry
1 medium egg, beaten
1 tbsp demerara (turbinado) sugar

Preheat the oven to 200°C/400°F/gas 6. Have ready two non-stick baking trays or line two trays with baking parchment.

Melt the butter in a medium saucepan and tip in the pecans. Fry the pecans for 1–2 minutes, until the butter is beginning to turn golden. Add the apple and sugar and cook gently, stirring occasionally, for 10–15 minutes, until the apple has mostly broken down and the liquid has evaporated. Set the mixture aside and leave to cool. Alternatively, make up the mixture the night before and refrigerate until ready to use.

Lightly dust a work surface with flour and lay the puff pastry sheet out over it. Cut the pastry into 6 equal squares. Spoon a sixth of the filling into one triangular half of each square, leaving a 1cm (½in) gap around the edge. Brush the edge with a little of the beaten egg and fold the other corner over the apple. Press a fork around the edge to seal. Brush the tops of the turnovers with the egg and sprinkle over the demerara sugar.

Divide the turnovers between the baking trays, leaving a 3–4cm (1½–1¾in) gap between each one, and bake for 10–12 minutes, until the turnovers are crisp and golden. Set aside to cool for 3–4 minutes, before removing from the tray and transferring to a wire rack to cool completely. The turnovers can be eaten warm or at room temperature and will keep in an airtight container for up to 2 days.

Salted almond and chocolate brittle

SERVES 12–15

200g (1⅔ cups) blanched almonds, roughly chopped

250g (1¼ cups) caster (superfine) sugar

125g (½ cup, plus 1 tbsp) unsalted butter, plus extra for greasing

½ tsp sea salt flakes

150g (1 cup) good-quality dark (bitter-sweet) chocolate, chopped into small pieces

Lightly grease and line a 30 x 20cm (12 x 8in) baking tray with baking parchment. Spread the almonds out on the parchment in an even layer.

Put the sugar, butter, salt and 100ml (⅔ cup) water into a saucepan and place over a low–medium heat. Stir the mixture until the butter has melted and the sugar has dissolved.

Once dissolved, increase the heat and boil the mixture for 5–10 minutes, until it has reached a golden caramel colour. Quickly and carefully pour the caramel over the almonds and set aside to cool completely.

Once the caramel is cool, melt the chocolate in a heatproof bowl set over a pan of barely simmering water, making sure the base of the bowl does not touch the water.

Invert the caramel on to a clean sheet of baking parchment so that the smooth side is uppermost. Pour over the chocolate and use a palette knife to spread it out evenly. Leave the chocolate to set completely before breaking into chunks to serve. The brittle can be stored in an airtight container, interleaved with baking parchment, for up to 2 days.

Elderflower and lemon cordial

2kg (4lb 6oz) granulated sugar
25 fresh elderflower heads

5 unwaxed lemons, 2 cut into slices; the juice of 3

Pour the sugar into a very large saucepan and add 1.5 litres (1½ quarts) of boiling water. Place the pan over a low heat and allow the sugar to dissolve, stirring occasionally. Bring the mixture to a boil, simmer for a couple of minutes, then remove from the heat.

Put the elderflower heads into a large bowl of water and gently wash the flowers to remove any dirt. Drain on a tea towel or cloth before adding to the syrup along with the lemon slices and juice. Cover the pan and leave to infuse in a cool place for 24 hours.

Strain the syrup through some muslin and use a funnel to fill sterilised bottles (see page 27 for how to sterilise). The cordial will keep in the fridge for up to a month.

(pictured overleaf)

Rose lemonade

MAKES 1 LITRE (1 QUART)

4½ unwaxed lemons
75g (6 tbsp) golden caster (superfine) sugar
750ml (3¼ cups) cold water

3 tbsp rose water
2 tsp dried rose petals (optional)
few drops of pink food colouring (optional)

Cut one of the lemons into chunks, removing any pips, and juice the remaining 3½.

Tip the chopped lemon and juice into a food processor along with the sugar and blitz until smooth. Add the water, rose water and rose petals, if using, and process again. If the lemonade is still quite chunky, strain before serving. If you want a very pink lemonade add a couple of drops of the food colouring, otherwise simply serve over ice. The lemonade will keep in the fridge for up to 2 days.

(pictured overleaf)

Berry cheesecake jars

120g (1 cup) digestive biscuits
40g (3 tbsp) unsalted butter, melted
200g (1 cup) cream cheese
1 tsp vanilla extract

200ml (1 cup) double (heavy) cream
40g (4½ tbsp) icing (powdered) sugar
400g (14oz) mixed berries

Break up the biscuits and pulse in a food processor until they resemble breadcrumbs. Alternatively, just put them into a freezer bag and bash them with a rolling pin. Transfer to a mixing bowl and pour over the melted butter. Stir until well combined before dividing between six 350ml (1½ cup) jars or glasses.

Spoon the cream cheese into a clean mixing bowl and beat with a whisk until smooth. Add the vanilla and cream, then sift over 30g (3½ tablespoons) of the icing sugar. Beat the mixture until soft, pillowy peaks have formed.

Lightly crush the berries with the back of a fork and stir through the remainder of the icing sugar. Ripple half of the berries through the cream, then divide this mixture between the jars. Top with the remaining berries. Screw the lids on to the jars to make them easy to transport or, if using glasses, cover with foil or cling film (plastic wrap). The cheesecakes can be kept refrigerated for up to 1 day before serving.

Apricot and raspberry jam tarts

MAKES 24

225g (1¾ cups) plain (all-purpose) flour, plus extra to dust
100g (½ cup, minus 1 tbsp) unsalted butter
2 tbsp caster (superfine) sugar

1 medium egg yolk
12 tsp good-quality apricot jam
12 tsp good-quality raspberry jam

Preheat the oven to 190°C/375°F/gas 5. Have ready two 12-hole jam tart tins (or bake the tarts in two batches).

Sift the flour into a mixing bowl. Using your fingertips, rub the butter into the flour until the mixture resembles breadcrumbs. Alternatively, whizz in a food processor.

Stir in the caster sugar and the egg yolk. Add 1–2 tablespoons of cold water and quickly mix to form a firm dough. Wrap in cling film (plastic wrap) and chill in the fridge for 30 minutes.

Lightly dust a work surface with flour and gently roll out the pastry until it is 2–3mm (⅛in) thick. Use a cutter slightly larger than the holes in the tart tin (usually about 6cm (2½in)) to cut out discs of pastry and line each hole in the tin. Working very lightly, re-roll any pieces of leftover pastry and continue to stamp out discs until all of the pastry has been used up.

Fill each pastry case with a teaspoon of apricot or raspberry jam and bake in the oven for 10–12 minutes – until the pastry is lightly golden and crisp. Allow to cool in the tin for 10 minutes before transferring to a wire rack to cool completely. The tarts can be kept in an airtight container for 3–4 days.

School fêtes
and bake sales

School fêtes and bake sales

A school fête or bake sale is a great way to get children helping out in the kitchen, so with that in mind many of the recipes in this chapter are simple enough for little helpers to get involved. From stirring the flapjack mixture to picking out their favourite ingredients for the marshmallow toffee squares and chocolate tiffin, children can get stuck in and feel proud that they've contributed to the bakes they take to school.

And we haven't neglected the adult buyers at your bake sale! There are aromatic lavender and orange and zesty lemon curd biscuits, a fruity lemon and blueberry traybake and a sumptuous millonaire's shortbread. These bakes have all been designed to cater to more grown-up palates, but are easy to pack into tins and transport in single portions. Pile them on to cake stands and pretty plates and wait for the sales rush to begin!

Millionaire's shortbread

MAKES 18 SQUARES

For the shortbread

185g (¾ cup, plus 2 tsp) cold, unsalted butter, cut into cubes, plus extra for greasing

50g (¼ cup) caster (superfine) sugar

250g (1¾ cups, plus 2 tbsp) plain (all-purpose) flour

For the caramel

150g (⅔ cup) unsalted butter

150g (¾ cup) golden caster (superfine) sugar

1 x 400g (14oz) can condensed milk

85g (¼ cup) golden syrup

pinch of salt

For the chocolate topping

150g (1 cup) good-quality dark (bitter-sweet) chocolate, chopped into small pieces

150g (1 cup) good-quality milk chocolate, chopped into small pieces

50g (⅓ cup) good-quality white chocolate, chopped into small pieces

Preheat the oven to 180°C/350°F/gas 4. Grease and line a deep 27 x 18cm (11 x 7in) baking tin (the depth needs to be at least 3cm (1½in).

To make the shortbread, beat the butter and sugar until pale and fluffy. Fold through the flour to make a fairly stiff dough. Tip the dough into the prepared tin and press into an even layer. Prick all over with a fork and transfer to the oven. Bake for 15–20 minutes, until pale golden and sandy in texture. Remove from the oven and set aside to cool in its tin.

Now make the caramel. Tip the butter, sugar, condensed milk and golden syrup into a heavy-based saucepan and place over a low heat. Stir continuously until the sugar has completely dissolved. At this point turn the heat up and bring the mixture to the boil, continuing to stir, until it is fairly thick and has taken on a caramel colour – this will take about 5 minutes. Stir through the salt, then immediately pour the caramel over the shortbread. Set aside on a wire rack for an hour (still in its tin), until the caramel has set.

For the topping, melt the dark and milk chocolate in a heatproof bowl set over a pan of barely simmering water, making sure the base of the bowl does not touch the water. As soon as it has melted, remove the bowl from the heat and pour the chocolate over the caramel. Use a palette knife to smooth it out evenly and allow to cool and set completely.

Place a clean heatproof bowl over a pan of simmering water and allow the white chocolate to melt in the same way. Drizzle it over the shortbread and allow to set for 10–15 minutes.

Cut the shortbread into squares to serve. The shortbread can be kept in an airtight container for up to a week.

Tip

If you're taking these to a bake sale, try to slice them at the event to stop the biscuit layers knocking together and crumbling during the journey.

Figgy flapjacks

MAKES 16

140g (⅔ cup) unsalted butter, plus extra for greasing
100g (½ cup) soft light brown sugar
4 tbsp golden syrup

250g (2½ cups) porridge oats (oatmeal)
150g (1 cup) soft dried figs, roughly chopped
50g (⅓ cup) pumpkin seeds

Preheat the oven to 180°C/350°F/gas 4. Lightly grease and line a 26 x 20cm (10½ x 8in) baking tin with baking parchment.

Tip the butter, sugar and golden syrup into a medium saucepan and melt over a low–medium heat, stirring often. When the sugar has completely dissolved, pour in the oats, figs and pumpkin seeds and stir until everything is well combined.

Pour the mixture into the prepared tin and smooth out until you have an even layer. Transfer the tin to the oven and bake for 20-25 minutes, until golden and fairly crisp on top. Leave to cool in the tin. When the flapjack is completely cool, use a sharp knife to cut it into 16 equal pieces. The flapjacks can be kept in an airtight container for up to a week.

Marshmallow toffee squares

200g (7oz) soft butter toffees
125g (½ cup, plus 1 tbsp) unsalted butter

200g (5½ cups) marshmallows
175g (7 cups) puffed rice cereal

Grease then line a 30 x 20cm (12 x 8in) baking tin with baking parchment.

Tip the toffees into a large, deep saucepan and add the butter and marshmallows. Place over a low heat and stir until everything has dissolved. Pour in the puffed rice cereal and stir until it is completely covered in the mallowy caramel.

Quickly spoon the mixture into the prepared tin and use the back of a spoon to smooth it out into an even layer. Set aside for up to 1 hour, until completely cool and set, then cut into 24 squares. The squares will keep in an airtight container for up to a week.

Pistachio and triple chocolate brownies

MAKES 16

180g (¾ cup, plus 2 tsp) unsalted butter, plus extra for greasing

150g (1 cup) good-quality dark (bittersweet) chocolate, chopped into small pieces

100g (⅔ cup) good-quality milk chocolate, chopped into small pieces

3 large eggs, beaten

200g (1 cup) soft light brown sugar

100g (½ cup) caster (superfine) sugar

90g (⅔ cup) plain (all-purpose) flour

40g (½ cup) cocoa powder

50g (⅓ cup) good-quality white chocolate, chopped into small pieces

50g (2oz) pistachio nuts, roughly chopped

Preheat the oven to 180°C/350°F/gas 4. Lightly grease and line a 20 x 20cm (8 x 8in) brownie tin with baking parchment.

Melt the butter, dark chocolate and 50g (⅓ cup) of the milk chocolate in a medium-sized, heatproof bowl set over a pan of barely simmering water, making sure the base of the bowl doesn't touch the water. As soon as the chocolate and butter have melted, remove the bowl from the heat and set aside to cool slightly.

Meanwhile, beat the eggs and sugars together until thickened and pale – this should take up to 5 minutes. Pour the chocolate mixture into the egg and sugar and very gently fold through until just combined. Sift over the flour and cocoa powder and fold these through, until just combined. Finally carefully fold in the remaining milk chocolate, the white chocolate and the pistachios, until they are well distributed through the mixture.

Spoon the brownie mix into the prepared tin and use the back of a spoon to smooth it out. Bake for 20–25 minutes, until the brownie has a crisp, sugary crust and is just set. Leave the brownie in its tin placed on a wire rack to cool. The brownies are delicious served warm but will keep in an airtight container for up to 3 days. Brownies tend to go stale more quickly if cut in advance of serving so cut these into squares just before eating.

Coconut and chocolate macaroons

MAKES 25–30

2 medium egg whites
100g (½ cup) caster (superfine) sugar
200g (2⅔ cup) desiccated coconut
pinch of salt

1 tsp vanilla extract
80g (½ cup) good-quality dark (bitter-sweet) chocolate

Whisk the egg whites in a medium bowl until soft peaks form. Continue to beat while adding the sugar a tablespoon at a time. Stir through the coconut, salt and vanilla and set aside for 20 minutes.

Preheat the oven to 160°C/325° F/gas 3. Line two baking sheets with baking parchment.

Using wet hands, roll the coconut mixture into walnut-sized balls and place on the baking sheets. Transfer to the oven and bake for 12–15 minutes, until the macaroons are just beginning to turn golden. Remove from the oven and set aside to cool completely.

Line a baking tray with a clean sheet of parchment. Melt the chocolate in a heatproof bowl set over a pan of barely simmering water, making sure the base of the bowl doesn't touch the water. As soon as the chocolate has melted, remove the bowl from the heat.

Dip each macaroon halfway into the melted chocolate and place on the lined tray to set. Repeat until all of the macaroons have been dipped. Any remaining chocolate can be drizzled over the top. The macaroons can be kept in an airtight container for up to 4 days.

Lemon and blueberry traybake

SERVES 12

200g (¾ cup, plus 2 tbsp) unsalted butter,
plus extra for greasing
200g (1 cup) caster (superfine) sugar
4 medium eggs, lightly beaten
200g (1½ cups) self-raising flour
1 tsp baking powder
finely grated zest and juice of 1 lemon
250g (2 cups) blueberries

For the icing
100g (¾ cup) icing (powdered) sugar
finely grated zest of 1 lemon, plus the
juice of ½

Preheat the oven to 180°C/350°F/gas 4. Lightly grease a 26 x 20cm (10½ x 8in) baking tin and line it with baking parchment.

Place the butter in a large mixing bowl, add the sugar and beat until pale and fluffy. Gradually add the egg, beating well between each addition.

Sift over the flour and baking powder and gently fold into the batter, until just combined. Stir through the lemon zest, juice and 200g (1½ cups) of the blueberries until well dispersed, before spooning the mixture into the prepared tin. Smooth the mixture with the back of a spoon then bake in the oven for 20–25 minutes, until lightly golden and a skewer inserted into the centre comes out clean. Set the cake aside to cool while you make the icing.

Sift the icing sugar into a mixing bowl and add a couple of teaspoons of the lemon juice. Gradually mix the sugar into the lemon juice, adding a little more juice as necessary, until you have a fairly runny mixture. Stir through the lemon zest then drizzle over the cake. Scatter over the remaining blueberries and cut into squares to serve. This will keep in an airtight container for up to 2 days (without the blueberries on top).

Peanut butter and chocolate chip cookies

MAKES 20–24

125g (½ cup, plus 1 tbsp) unsalted butter, at room temperature
125g (½ cup) crunchy peanut butter
200g (1 cup) soft light brown sugar
80g (7 tbsp) caster (superfine) sugar
2 medium eggs, lightly beaten
2 tbsp golden syrup
1 tsp vanilla extract
2 tbsp milk

325g (2½ scant cups) plain (all-purpose) flour
1 tsp bicarbonate of soda (baking soda)
100g (⅔ cup) good-quality dark (bitter-sweet) chocolate, roughly chopped
100g (⅔ cup) good-quality milk chocolate, roughly chopped
30g (¼ cup) roasted and salted peanuts, roughly chopped

Preheat the oven to 180°C/350°F/gas 4. Line two baking sheets with baking parchment.

Beat the butter, peanut butter and sugars until light and fluffy. Gradually add the egg, beating well after each addition.

Stir in the golden syrup, vanilla and milk, then sift over the flour and bicarbonate of soda. Fold these through to create a stiff dough. Stir through the chocolate and peanuts until well dispersed.

Using an ice-cream scoop or tablespoon, spoon heaps of the dough on to the prepared baking sheets, ensuring that each mound is roughly 7cm (3in) away from the next – the cookies will spread. Bake for 10–12 minutes, until golden, then remove from the oven.

Allow the cookies to cool on the baking sheets for 5–10 minutes, before transferring to a wire rack to cool completely. The cookies can be kept in an airtight container for up to 3 days; they can also be frozen and warmed through in an oven preheated to 110°C/225°F/gas ¼ for 10 minutes.

Lemon curd biscuits

MAKES ABOUT 30

200g (¾ cup, plus 2 tbsp) unsalted butter
200g (1 cup) golden caster (superfine) sugar
1 medium egg, beaten
220g (1⅔ cups) plain (all-purpose) flour

50g (½ cup) ground almonds
½ tsp baking powder
finely grated zest of 1 lemon
½ x 325g (12oz) jar good-quality lemon curd

Preheat the oven to 180°C/350°F/gas 4. Line two large baking sheets with baking parchment.

Beat the butter and sugar together until light and fluffy, then beat in the egg.

Fold in the flour, ground almonds, baking powder and lemon zest to create a fairly stiff dough. Roll the dough into 30 equal-sized balls, about 2–3cm (¾–1in) in diameter. Divide the balls between the baking sheets, ensuring that they are at least 5cm (2in) apart. Use your thumb to create a deep imprint in the centre of each cookie and fill each with ¼–½ teaspoon of lemon curd.

Transfer the sheets to the oven and bake for 10–12 minutes, until the biscuits are pale golden and the curd is bubbling. Transfer to a wire rack to cool completely before serving. The biscuits will keep in an airtight container for up to 3 days.

(pictured overleaf)

Lavender and orange biscuits

MAKES ABOUT 32

300g (2¼ cups) plain (all-purpose) flour, plus extra to dust
180g (¾ cup, plus 2 tsp) unsalted butter, at room temperature, cut into cubes
110g (½ cup, plus 1 tbsp) caster (superfine) sugar

finely grated zest of 2 oranges
1½ tsp edible dried lavender
2 medium egg yolks

Tip the flour and butter into the bowl of a food processor and pulse until the mixture resembles breadcrumbs.

Add the remaining ingredients and process until the mixture just forms a ball of dough. Remove from the processor, shape the dough into a disc, wrap in cling film (plastic wrap) and chill for 30 minutes.

Preheat the oven to 180°C/350°F/gas 4. Line two baking sheets with parchment and set aside.

Lightly dust a work surface and rolling pin with flour and roll the dough out to a thickness of 1cm (½in). Using a 7cm (3in) cutter, stamp out as many biscuits as you can, before re-rolling the scraps and continuing to stamp out biscuits until all of the dough has been used.

Transfer the rounds to the prepared sheets and bake for 12–15 minutes, until pale golden with a sandy texture. Transfer to a wire rack to cool. These biscuits will keep in an airtight container for up to a week.

(pictured overleaf)

Party rings

MAKES ABOUT 36

150g (⅔ cup) unsalted butter, softened
250g (1¾ cups, plus 2 tbsp) plain (all-purpose) flour, plus extra to dust
50g (2oz) cornflour
125g (⅔ cup) caster (superfine) sugar

1 large egg
1 tsp vanilla extract
400g (3 cups) royal icing sugar
food colouring pastes of your choice

Tip the butter, flour and cornflour into a food processor. Pulse until the mixture resembles breadcrumbs, then add the sugar, egg and vanilla. Pulse again until the mixture just forms a rough ball and tip it out on to a lightly floured work surface. Bring the dough together, without kneading, to form a disc. Wrap the disc in cling film (plastic wrap) and refrigerate for 30 minutes.

Preheat the oven to 180°C/350°F/gas 4. Line two baking sheets with baking parchment.

Lightly flour a work surface and gently roll out the biscuit dough until it is 2-3mm (⅛in) thick. Use a 6cm (2½in) fluted cutter to cut out as many rounds as possible, before using a 2cm (¾in) cutter to stamp and remove a central hole from the middle. Gather and bind any scraps of dough, them roll them out and cut out more biscuits. Transfer to the baking sheets and bake for 10-12 minutes, until pale golden. Leave on the baking sheets for 5 minutes, before transferring to a wire rack to cool completely.

When the biscuits are cool make the icing by sifting the icing sugar into a large bowl. Add a few teaspoons of freshly boiled water and gradually whisk to create a paste. Add a little more water until you achieve a spreadable consistency. Separate the icing into several bowls and mix a tiny amount of a different colour into each until you have your desired colours. To decorate the biscuits, use a small palette knife to spread a layer of icing over each one. Holding a biscuit between your fingertips, use a teaspoon to pick up a small amount of a contrasting coloured icing and quickly and carefully drizzle 3-4 lines over the biscuit starting at the side furthest from you and drawing it towards you. Turn the biscuit by 90 degrees and draw a cocktail stick through the lines to feather the icing. Place on a clean baking sheet and leave to set. Repeat with the remaining biscuits. These can be stored in an airtight container for up to 3 weeks.

Peach Melba streusel slices

MAKES 16

For the streusel

100g (¾ cup) plain (all-purpose) flour

75g (⅓ cup) unsalted butter, at room temperature, cut into small cubes

40g (3 tbsp) demerara (turbinado) sugar

25g (2 tbsp) flaked almonds

For the cake

200g (¾ cup, plus 2 tbsp) unsalted butter, at room temperature, plus extra for greasing

200g (1 cup) caster (superfine) sugar

4 medium eggs, beaten

175g (1⅓ cups) self-raising flour

1 tsp baking powder

50g (½ cup) ground almonds

1 tsp vanilla extract

2 ripe peaches, halved, stoned and cut into 5mm (¼in) wedges

150g (1¼ cups) raspberries

Preheat the oven to 180°C/350°F/gas 4. Grease and line a 20cm (8in) square baking tin with baking parchment.

Begin by making the streusel. Tip the flour and butter into a bowl and using your fingertips, rub the butter into the flour until the mixture forms clumps and no lumps of butter remain. Stir through the sugar and almonds and place in the fridge until needed.

For the cake, beat the butter and sugar until pale and fluffy. Gradually add the egg, beating well between each addition. Sift over the flour and baking powder and sprinkle over the ground almonds, breaking up any lumps as you go. Fold through until just combined, before gently stirring through the vanilla, until just incorporated. Spoon the mixture into the prepared tin and smooth out into an even layer. Lay the peach slices over the cake and scatter over the raspberries, followed by the streusel topping. Transfer to the oven and bake for 50 minutes to 1 hour, until the cake has risen and a skewer inserted into the centre comes out clean. Check the cake after 35 minutes; if the top is getting quite golden, cover with foil and return it to the oven. Leave the cake to cool in its tin before removing and cutting into squares. The cake can be kept in an airtight container for up to 2 days.

Malted chocolate cookies

MAKES 16

160g (¾ cup, minus 2 tsp) unsalted butter
125g (⅔ cup) soft light brown sugar
50g (¼ cup) caster (superfine) sugar
2 medium eggs, beaten
200g (1½ cups) plain (all-purpose) flour
175g (1¾ cups) malted milk powder

½ tsp bicarbonate of soda (baking soda)
pinch of salt
150g (5oz) chocolate-coated honeycomb balls, roughly crushed (you need the pieces to stay chunky)
50g (⅓ cup) good-quality milk chocolate, roughly chopped

Preheat the oven to 180°C/350°F/gas 4. Line two large baking sheets with baking parchment.

Beat the butter and sugars together until light and fluffy. Gradually add the egg, beating well after each addition.

Fold through the flour, malted milk, bicarbonate of soda and salt to form a sticky but firm dough. Stir through the chocolate-coated honeycomb balls and chocolate until well dispersed.

Use an ice-cream scoop or tablespoon to spoon heaps of the mixture on to the prepared baking sheets, ensuring that they are spaced at least 8cm (3in) apart. Transfer to the oven and bake for 10–12 minutes until golden. Allow the cookies to set on the baking sheets for at least 5 minutes before transferring to a wire rack to cool completely. The cookies will keep in an airtight container for up to 3 days.

Cranberry and pistachio tiffin

300g (2 cups) good-quality milk chocolate, chopped into small pieces

100g (⅔ cup) good-quality dark (bitter-sweet) chocolate, chopped into small pieces

4 tbsp golden syrup

100g (½ cup, minus 1 tbsp) unsalted butter

200g (1⅔ cups) digestive biscuits, broken into small pieces

100g (⅔ cup) shelled pistachio nuts

100g (⅔ cup) dried cranberries

50g (⅓ cup) good-quality white chocolate

Line a 20cm (8in) square baking tin with baking parchment.

Place both chocolates, the golden syrup and butter in a heatproof bowl set over a pan of barely simmering water, making sure the base of the bowl does not touch the water, and allow to melt. Remove the bowl from the heat and set aside to cool slightly.

Put a clean heatproof bowl back over the pan of simmering water and tip in the white chocolate. Leave to melt.

Meanwhile, stir the biscuit, pistachios and cranberries into the melted syrup mixture then spoon it into the prepared tin. Spread the mixture out evenly and drizzle over the white chocolate. Chill in the fridge for at least 2 hours before cutting into squares. The tiffin can be kept covered in the fridge for 3–4 days.

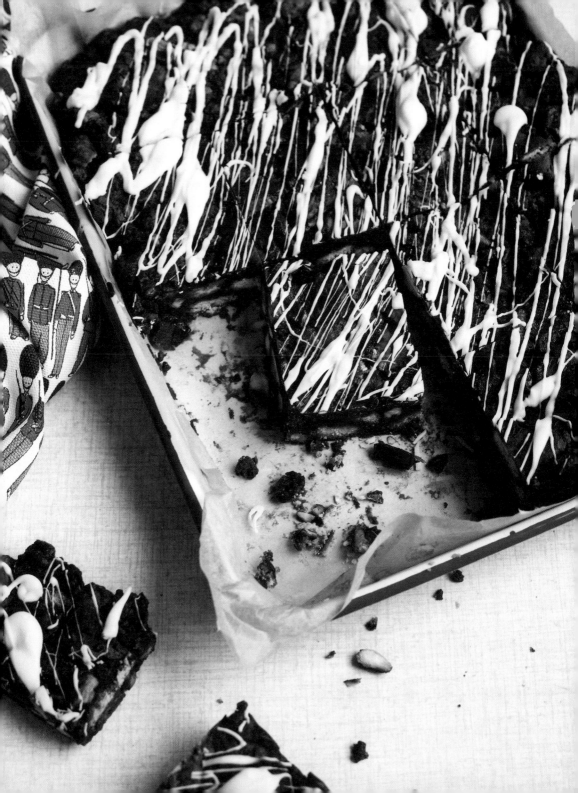

Celebration cakes

Celebration cakes

As elaborate and beautifully decorated as shop-bought cakes can be, there's something very special about baking your own cake to mark a celebration. Nothing quite rivals the flavour of a home-made cake and the thought behind it really shows that you care.

Celebration cakes don't have to be complicated works of art. The recipes in this chapter are all elegant and inventive in flavour but you don't need a mastery of sugar sculpture to make them stand out. There's something for everyone and every occasion: from a decadent, dark chocolate cake with an Earl Grey ganache and a chocolate orange marble cake with orange buttercream for the chocolate lover in your life, to a light and summery Eton mess cake and a festive spiced fig and cinnamon cake so you can match your bake to the season. With advice on how to make the creamiest buttercream and tips for wowing your guests with simple decoration techniques, you can be sure your celebration cake will dazzle and delight.

Chocolate, Earl Grey and lavender cake

175g (1 cup) good-quality dark (bitter-sweet) chocolate (70 per cent cocoa solids), roughly chopped

200g (¾ cup, plus 2 tbsp) unsalted butter, plus extra for greasing

100g (¾ cup) self-raising flour

70g (½ cup, plus ½ tbsp) plain (all-purpose) flour

¼ tsp bicarbonate of soda (baking soda)

30g (⅓ cup) cocoa powder

200g (1 cup) caster (superfine) sugar

175g (6oz) soft light brown sugar

3 medium eggs, lightly beaten

75ml (⅓ cup) buttermilk

For the Earl Grey ganache

200g (1¼ cups) good-quality dark (bitter-sweet) chocolate (70 per cent cocoa solids), roughly chopped

300ml (1¼ cups) double (heavy) cream

4 tsp Earl Grey tea leaves

1 tsp edible dried lavender

2 tbsp caster (superfine) sugar

Preheat the oven to 160°C/325°F/gas 3. Grease and line a 18cm (7in) loose-bottomed tin with baking parchment.

Place the chocolate and butter in a small saucepan. Add 100ml (½ cup) cold water and place over a low heat, stirring occasionally, until the chocolate has just melted. Remove from the heat and leave to cool slightly. Meanwhile, sift the flours, bicarbonate of soda, cocoa powder and sugars into a large bowl. Beat the eggs and buttermilk together in a measuring jug.

Pour the chocolate mixture into the dry mixture then pour in the eggs and buttermilk and gently fold everything together until just incorporated. Pour into the tin and bake for 1¼ –1½ hours, until a skewer inserted into the centre of the cake comes out clean. Leave the cake to cool in its tin for 1 hour before turning out on to a wire rack to cool completely.

Once the cake is cool, make the ganache. Place the chocolate in a large mixing bowl. Pour the cream into a small pan and stir through the tea leaves and lavender. Place the cream over a low heat for 5 minutes, stirring, until warmed through. Remove from the heat and leave to infuse for 15 minutes.

Once the cream has infused, bring it to a simmer over a low heat, stir through the sugar until dissolved, then pour the hot cream through a sieve over the chocolate. Using small circular motions, stir the cream from the middle of the bowl, gradually incorporating the chocolate until you have a smooth, shiny mixture.

Cut the cake into two or three even layers and use a palette knife to sandwich them together with a thin layer of ganache. Dollop half of the remaining ganache on top of the cake and using the palette knife, gradually work it out to the edge of the cake. Spread the remainder around the sides of the cake and smooth it around as evenly as you can. Allow the ganache to set for 10 minutes before serving. This cake will stay moist for up to 3 days if kept in an airtight container.

Eton mess layer cake

SERVES 12

300g (1⅓ cups) unsalted butter	1 tsp baking powder
300g (1½ cups) caster (superfine) sugar	1½ tsp vanilla extract
4 medium eggs, lightly beaten	400ml (1¾ cups) double (heavy) cream
200g (1½ cups) self-raising flour	16 shop-bought mini meringue shells
100g (1 cup) ground almonds	400g (14 oz) mixed summer berries

Preheat the oven to 180°C/350°F/gas 4. Grease and line three 20cm (8in) sandwich tins with baking parchment.

Beat the butter and sugar together until very pale and fluffy in texture. Gradually add the egg, beating well after each addition. Sift over the flour, ground almonds and baking powder and gently fold through the mixture until just combined. Stir through 1 teaspoon of the vanilla, before dividing the mixture between the three tins and smoothing the tops.

Transfer the tins to the oven and bake for 30–35 minutes, until the cakes are well risen and a skewer inserted into the centre comes out clean. Allow the cakes to cool in their tins for 10 minutes, before turning out on to a wire rack to cool completely.

To assemble the cake, lightly whip the cream with the remaining vanilla until it is just beginning to form soft peaks. Roughly crush 10 of the meringues and lightly stir them through the cream.

Place one of the cake layers on to a serving plate or cake board and spread over a third of the cream. Sprinkle over a third of the berries and repeat with the remaining layers of cake. Top with the remaining meringues to serve.

Lemon and rosemary cake

SERVES 8

275g (1¼ cups, minus 2 tsp) unsalted butter, plus extra for greasing

325g (1½ cups, plus 2 tbsp) golden caster (superfine) sugar

4 medium eggs, lightly beaten

175g (1¾ cups) ground almonds

75g (⅔ cup) gluten-free flour

1½ tsp gluten-free baking powder

grated zest and juice of 2 lemons

5 rosemary sprigs, plus extra to decorate

100g (¾ cup, minus ½ tbsp) icing (powdered) sugar

Preheat the oven to 180°C/350°F/gas 4. Grease and line a deep 18cm (7in) cake tin with baking parchment.

Beat the butter and 275g (1½ cups, minus 2 tbsp) of the sugar until pale and fluffy. Beat in the egg, a little at a time, beating well after each addition. Sprinkle over the ground almonds, breaking up any lumps as you go. Sift over the flour and baking powder, add the lemon zest and fold in until just combined. Scrape the mixture into the tin. Bake for 45–50 minutes, until the cake is well risen and a skewer inserted into the centre comes out clean.

While the cake is baking, make the syrup. Add the remaining caster sugar and the juice of one of the lemons to a small saucepan. Add the rosemary and place over a low–medium heat to dissolve the sugar. Once dissolved, turn the heat up and simmer for 3–4 minutes, until it reaches a syrupy consistency. Set aside to cool slightly.

As soon as the cake comes out of the oven, use a cocktail stick to make small holes over the surface. Strain the syrup and pour it evenly over the cake. Allow the cake to cool in its tin for 10 minutes, before turning out on to a wire rack to cool completely.

To make the icing, sift the icing sugar into a mixing bowl. Pour in the remaining lemon juice and gradually stir it into the sugar until it is a fairly runny consistency (adjust with water if it is too thick). Pour the icing over the cake and sprinkle over a few extra bits of rosemary to serve.

Strawberry and coconut cake

225g (1 cup) unsalted butter

225g (1 cup, plus ½ tbsp) caster (superfine) sugar

4 medium eggs, lightly beaten

225g (1¾ cups) self-raising flour

½ tsp baking powder

1 tsp vanilla extract

100g (1⅓ cups) desiccated coconut, plus an extra 2 tbsp, to decorate

For the buttercream

40g (1½oz) freeze-dried strawberries

300g (1⅓ cups) unsalted butter, at room temperature

600g (4¼ cups) icing (powdered) sugar

200g (1½ cups) fresh strawberries, finely sliced

Preheat the oven to 180°C/350°F/gas 4. Grease and line two 20cm (8in) sandwich tins with baking parchment.

Beat the butter and sugar together until pale and fluffy. Gradually beat in the beaten eggs, a little at a time, beating well after each addition. Sift over the flour and baking powder and gently fold into the mixture until just combined. Add the vanilla and coconut and gently stir through. Divide the mixture between the prepared tins, smoothing the tops with a palette knife or spatula. Bake for 25–30 minutes, until the cakes are golden and a skewer inserted into the centre comes out clean.

Transfer the cakes to a wire rack and leave to cool completely. Once cool, use a bread knife to carefully slice each cake into two even layers. Set aside.

To make the buttercream, place the freeze-dried strawberries in a food processor and blitz to a powder (you could also pound them using a pestle and mortar). In a large bowl, beat the butter until soft, then add a third of the icing sugar and beat until the mixture is crumb-like. Add another third of the sugar, beat again and when the sugar is incorporated, beat in the remainder, along with the strawberry powder. Mix until light and fluffy.

Pile 5–6 tablespoons of the buttercream on to one of the cake layers. Using a palette knife, smooth it evenly to the edges of the cake and top with a

third of the sliced strawberries, arranging them in as even and flat a layer as possible. Repeat these layers until all of the cakes are stacked up (the top cake won't have any buttercream or strawberries on it).

Smooth the remaining buttercream over the top and sides of the cake and decorate the top with the extra desiccated coconut to serve.

Pear and
salted caramel cake

SERVES 12

200g (¾ cup, plus 2 tbsp) unsalted butter, plus extra for greasing

125g (⅔ cup, minus 2 tsp) caster sugar

75g (6 tbsp) soft light brown sugar

4 medium eggs, lightly beaten

200g (1½ cups) self-raising flour

1 tsp baking powder

1 tsp vanilla extract

For the pears

500g (2½ cups) golden caster (superfine) sugar

pared zest of 1 lemon

4 cloves

1 cinnamon stick

1 litre (1 quart) boiling water

4 ripe pears

For the icing

200g (¾ cup, plus 2 tbsp) unsalted butter, at room temperature

400g (2 cups) soft light brown sugar

125ml (½ cup) full-fat milk

1 tsp sea salt, or more to taste

4 tbsp double (heavy) cream

350g (2½ cups) icing (powdered) sugar

50g (¼ cup) cream cheese

Begin by poaching the pears. Place the sugar, lemon zest, cloves and cinnamon in a large saucepan and pour in the boiling water from the kettle. Place over a low-medium heat and stir gently to dissolve the sugar. Once the sugar has dissolved, peel the pears and pop them in the pan. Cover with a lid and simmer gently for 30 minutes, until the pears are soft enough for a table knife to go through them, but not mushy. Carefully lift the pears out of the syrup and set aside to cool. Alternatively, leave the pears in the syrup overnight if you wish to get ahead.

Preheat the oven to 180°C/350°F/gas 4. Grease and line two 20cm (8in) sandwich tins with baking parchment. To make the cake, beat the butter and sugars together until pale and fluffy. Gradually beat in the egg, a little at a time, beating well after each addition. Sift over the flour and baking powder and gently fold into the mixture until just combined. Add the vanilla and

gently stir through until combined. Divide the mixture between the tins, smoothing the tops, and bake for 25–30 minutes, until the cakes are golden and a skewer inserted into the centre comes out clean. Leave the cakes to cool in their tins for 10 minutes, then turn them out on to a wire rack to cool completely.

To make the icing, place the butter and brown sugar in a saucepan over a low heat. Stir until the sugar has melted, at which point turn the heat up slightly and allow the mixture to bubble for 2 minutes. Carefully pour in the milk and stir to combine. Stir through the salt, remove from the heat and set aside to cool to room temperature.

Once cooled, pour 125ml (½ cup) of the sauce into a bowl and add the cream to it, stirring. Taste and add a little more salt if necessary, then set aside.

Once the remaining caramel has cooled completely, pour it into a mixing bowl and beat for 2 minutes to thicken it slightly. Sift over half of the icing sugar and beat it into the mixture. Add the remaining icing sugar and beat until light and fluffy. Stir through the cream cheese (do not beat as it will loosen the mixture) and set aside.

To assemble the cake, cut all but one or two of the poached pears in half lengthways (reserve the whole ones(s) for decoration) and use a teaspoon to scoop out the core and seeds. Cut the pears into slices. Place one of the cake layers on to a serving plate or cake board and use a palette knife to smooth over half of the icing, almost to the edges. Top with the slices of pear and place the second cake layer on top. Smooth the remaining icing over the top of the cake and decorate with the remaining pear(s). Pour over the reserved caramel sauce and serve immediately.

Chocolate and raspberry cake

SERVES 12

200g (¾ cup, plus 2 tbsp) unsalted butter, plus extra for greasing

175g (¾ cup, plus 2 tbsp) caster (superfine) sugar

25g (2 tbsp) soft light brown sugar

4 medium eggs, beaten

180g (1⅓ cups) self-raising flour

20g (2 tbsp) cocoa powder

1 tsp baking powder

2–3 tbsp milk

For the buttercream

30g (2 tbsp) freeze-dried raspberries

200g (1¼ cups) white chocolate

250g (1 cup, plus 2 tbsp) unsalted butter, softened

250g (1¾ cups) icing (powdered) sugar

300g (2½ cups) fresh raspberries

Preheat the oven to 180°C/350°F/gas 4. Grease and line two 20cm (8in) sandwich tins with baking parchment.

Beat the butter and sugars together until very pale and fluffy. Gradually add the egg, beating well after each addition. Sift over the flour, cocoa powder and baking powder and gently fold through the mixture until just combined. Briefly stir through the milk to loosen the mixture a little before dividing between the tins and smoothing the tops.

Bake for 30–35 minutes, until the cakes are well risen and a skewer inserted in the centre comes out clean. Leave the cakes to cool in their tins for 10 minutes before turning out on to a wire rack to cool completely.

Once the cakes are completely cool, make the buttercream. Place the freeze-dried raspberries in a food processor and blitz to a powder. Set aside. Melt the white chocolate in a heatproof bowl set over a pan of barely simmering water, making sure the base of the bowl does not touch the water, then remove the bowl from the heat and set aside.

Beat the butter with half of the icing sugar until just combined. Sift over the remaining icing sugar, tip in the raspberry powder and beat again until light and fluffy. Pour in the chocolate and beat again until smooth. Place one of the cakes on a serving plate or cake board and spoon over a third of the buttercream. Scatter over half of the fresh raspberries and top with the second cake layer. Use a palette knife to smooth the remaining buttercream over the cake and decorate with the remaining raspberries to serve.

200g (¾ cup, plus 2 tbsp) unsalted butter, plus extra for greasing

175g (¾ cup, plus 2 tbsp) soft light brown sugar

4 medium eggs, lightly beaten

3 very ripe bananas, mashed

300g (2¼ cups) self-raising flour

1 tsp baking powder

1 tsp vanilla extract

50g (½ cup) pecans, finely chopped

For the buttercream

200g (¾ cup, plus 2 tbsp) unsalted butter, at room temperature

400g (2 cups) soft light brown sugar

125ml (½ cup) full-fat milk

400g (3 cups) icing (powdered) sugar

50g (¼ cup) mascarpone cheese

banana chips, to decorate

Preheat the oven to 180°C/350°F/gas 4. Grease and line two 20cm (8in) sandwich tins with baking parchment.

Beat the butter and sugar until pale and fluffy. Gradually beat in the egg, a little at a time, beating well after each addition. Stir through the banana, then sift over the flour and baking powder and gently fold into the mixture until just combined. Add the vanilla and pecans and stir through until combined.

Divide the mixture between the tins, smoothing the tops. Transfer to the oven and bake for 25–30 minutes, until the cakes are golden and a skewer inserted into the centre comes out clean. Allow the cakes to cool in their tins for 10 minutes before turning out on to a wire rack to cool completely.

To make the buttercream, place the butter and brown sugar in a saucepan set over a low heat. Stir until the butter has melted and the sugar has dissolved, then turn the heat up slightly, allow the mixture to come to a gentle boil and leave it to bubble for 2 minutes. Carefully pour in the milk and stir to combine. Remove the pan from the heat and set aside until the mixture – now a caramel – has cooled to room temperature.

Pour the caramel into a mixing bowl and beat for 2 minutes to thicken it slightly. Sift over half of the icing sugar and beat it into the mixture. Add the remaining icing sugar and beat it until light and fluffy. Briefly beat in the mascarpone until smooth.

To assemble, place one of the cakes on to a serving plate or cake board and smooth half the buttercream over it, right to the edge. Top with the second cake layer and smooth the remaining buttercream over the top. Decorate the top with the banana chips or see the tip below.

Tip

It's easy to take an everyday cake and add a bit of dazzle and sparkle for a celebration. Cookware shops and supermarkets have lots to offer the home baker, from edible glitter sprays and stardust to sugar roses and chocolate stars. Why not get creative and make your cakes look extra special?

275g (1¼ cups, minus 2 tsp) unsalted butter, plus extra for greasing

275g (1½ cups, minus 2 tbsp) caster (superfine) sugar

5 medium eggs, lightly beaten

250g (1¾ cups, plus 2 tbsp) self-raising flour

50g (½ cup) ground almonds

1 tsp baking powder

6 tbsp milk

grated zest of 1 orange

3 tbsp cocoa powder

For the buttercream

50g (⅓ cup) good-quality dark (bitter-sweet) chocolate (70 per cent cocoa solids), roughly chopped

100g (½ cup, minus 1 tbsp) unsalted butter, at room temperature

200g (1½ cups, minus 1 tbsp) icing (powdered) sugar

grated zest of 1 orange

Preheat the oven to 180°C/350°F/gas 4. Lightly grease a 1.5-litre (6 cup) Bundt tin and set aside.

Beat the butter and the sugar until pale and fluffy. Beat in the eggs, a little at a time, beating well after each addition. Sift over the flour, ground almonds and baking powder and fold until everything is just combined.

Add 5 tablespoons of the milk, along with the orange zest, and gently stir through the mixture. Spoon half of the mixture into a separate bowl. Sift the cocoa powder into one of the bowls, then pour over the remaining tablespoon of milk and fold it through until the mixture is smooth and the cocoa is evenly distributed.

Use separate spoons to dollop the separate cake batters into the tin alternately. When all of the cake mixture has been added, use a skewer to gently swirl the different colours and create a marbled effect.

Transfer the cake to the oven and bake for 50 minutes, or until the cake is well risen and a skewer inserted into the centre comes out clean. Allow the cake to cool in its tin for 10 minutes, before turning out on to a wire rack to cool completely.

To make the buttercream, melt the chocolate in a heatproof bowl over a pan of barely simmering water, making sure the base of the bowl does not touch the water. As soon as it has melted, remove the bowl from the heat and set aside to cool slightly.

Beat the butter with half of the icing sugar until smooth. Add the remaining icing sugar and beat until light and fluffy. Pour in the cooled chocolate, along with the orange zest, and beat again until smooth.

To decorate the cake, place it on a serving plate or cake board. Smooth the buttercream over the top of the cake before serving in slices.

200g (¾ cup, plus 2 tbsp) unsalted butter, plus extra for greasing

125g (2/3 cup, minus 2 tsp) caster (superfine) sugar

75g (6 tbsp) soft light brown sugar

4 medium eggs, lightly beaten

175g (1⅓ cups) self-raising flour

50g (½ cup) ground almonds

1½ tsp ground cinnamon

1 tsp baking powder

5 ripe figs, finely sliced

For the buttercream

200g (¾ cup, plus 2 tbsp) unsalted butter, at room temperature

300g (2 cups, plus 2 tbsp) icing (powdered) sugar

1 tsp vanilla extract

½ tsp ground cinnamon

juice of ½ lemon

few drops of pink food colouring

125g (1 cup) ready-to-eat soft dried figs, finely chopped

Preheat the oven to 180°C/350°F/gas 4. Grease and line two 20cm (8in) sandwich tins with baking parchment.

Beat the butter and sugars together until pale and fluffy. Gradually beat in the egg, a little at a time, beating well after each addition. Sift over the flour, ground almonds, cinnamon and baking powder and gently fold into the mixture until just combined. Divide the mixture between the tins, smoothing the tops, and bake for 30–35 minutes, until the cakes are golden and a skewer inserted into the centre comes out clean. Allow the cakes to cool in their tins for 10 minutes before transferring to a wire rack to cool completely.

To make the buttercream, beat the butter with half of the icing sugar until smooth. Add the remaining icing sugar and beat until light and fluffy. Add the vanilla, cinnamon, lemon juice and food colouring and beat again until smooth. Stir through the dried figs until well incorporated. To assemble, place one cake on a serving plate or cake board and smooth a third of the buttercream over it, right to the edge. Cover with most of the fresh fig slices, reserving some for decoration. Top with the other cake and smooth the remaining buttercream all over the cake. Decorate with the reserved figs.

225g (1 cup) unsalted butter, plus extra for greasing

225g (1 cup, plus 2 tbsp) soft light brown sugar

4 medium eggs, lightly beaten

175g (1 1/3 cups) self-raising flour

50g (1/2 cup) ground almonds

1 tsp baking powder

150ml (2/3 cup) strong coffee, cooled

For the buttercream

200g (3/4 cup, plus 2 tbsp) unsalted butter, at room temperature

400g (3 cups) icing (powdered) sugar

4 tbsp double (heavy) cream

2–3 tbsp coffee essence (depending on the strength desired)

cocoa powder, to dust

Preheat the oven to 180°C/350°F/gas 4. Grease and line two 20cm (8in) sandwich tins with baking parchment.

Beat the butter and sugar together until pale and fluffy. Gradually add the egg, a little at a time, beating well after each addition. Sift over the flour, ground almonds and baking powder and fold into the mixture until just combined. Carefully stir through the coffee and divide the mixture between the tins, smoothing the tops. Bake for 25–30 minutes, until the cakes are golden and a skewer inserted into the centre comes out clean.

Allow the cakes to cool in their tins for 10 minutes, before turning out on to a wire rack to cool completely.

To make the buttercream, beat the butter until soft. Add a third of the icing sugar and beat until the mixture is crumb-like. Add another third of the sugar, beat again and when combined beat in the remaining sugar. Beat until light and fluffy.

Beat in the cream and when smooth remove a quarter of the buttercream to a separate bowl and set aside. Add 2–3 tablespoons of the coffee essence (the amount depends on how strong you would like the coffee flavour) to the larger bowl of buttercream and beat thoroughly, until evenly distributed.

To assemble, pile a third of the buttercream on to one of the cakes. Smooth it evenly to the edges of the cake and top with the second layer. Cover the top and sides of the cake with the remaining coffee-flavoured buttercream and then dollop or spread the white buttercream on top to look like a frothy cappuccino. Dust with a little cocoa powder to serve.

Tip

If you can't get hold of coffee essence, simply replace it with 1–2 teaspoons of instant espresso powder dissolved in 1 tablespoon of hot water. Leave it to cool before beating into the buttercream.

Index

Cath Kidston® acknowledgements

Special thanks to everyone involved in the making of this book: to Elaine Ashton, Katie Buckingham, Sue Chidler, Jena Glover-Dickson, Natasha Hinds-Payne, Gemma Hurley, Victoria Kay, Elisabeth Lester, Lyndsey Nangle, Toni Stait and all at Cath Kidston Ltd.

Publishing Director: Sarah Lavelle
Creative Director: Helen Lewis
Editor: Imogen Fortes
Designer: Gemma Hayden
Photographer: Rita Platts
Recipe writer and food stylist: Emily Jonzen
Prop stylist: Holly Bruce
Production Manager: Stephen Lang
Production Director: Vincent Smith

First published in 2016 by
Quadrille Publishing
Pentagon House
52–54 Southwark Street
London SE1 1UN
www.quadrille.co.uk

Quadrille is an imprint of Hardie Grant
www.hardiegrant.com.au

Cataloguing in Publication Data: a catalogue record for this book is available from the British Library.

ISBN: 978 184949 805 0

Printed in China

For more Cath Kidston products, visit cathkidston.com